MAHATMA GANDHI
Fighting for Indian Independence

REBELS WITH A CAUSE

MAHATMA GANDHI
Fighting for Indian Independence

Eileen Lucas

 Enslow Publishing
101 W. 23rd Street
Suite 240
New York, NY 10011
USA

enslow.com

Published in 2018 by Enslow Publishing, LLC.
101 W. 23rd Street, Suite 240, New York, NY 10011

Library of Congress Cataloging-in-Publication Data

Names: Lucas, Eileen, author.
Title: Mahatma Gandhi : fighting for Indian independence / Eileen Lucas.
Description: New York : Enslow Publishing, 2018. | Series: Rebels with a cause | Audience: Grades 7 to 12. | Includes bibliographical references and index.
Identifiers: LCCN 2017003087 | ISBN 9780766085138 (library-bound)
Subjects: LCSH: Gandhi, Mahatma, 1869-1948–Juvenile literature. | Statesmen–India–Biography–Juvenile literature. | Nationalists–India–Biography–Juvenile literature. | Lawyers–India–Biography–Juvenile literature. | India–Politics and government–1919-1947–Juvenile literature. | South Africa–Politics and government–1836-1909–Juvenile literature.
Classification: LCC DS481.G3 L83 2018 | DDC 954.03/5092 [B]–dc23
LC record available at https://lccn.loc.gov/2017003087

Printed in the United States of America

To Our Readers: We have done our best to make sure all website addresses in this book were active and appropriate when we went to press. However, the author and the publisher have no control over and assume no liability for the material available on those websites or on any websites they may link to. Any comments or suggestions can be sent by email to customerservice@enslow.com.

Photo Credits: Cover, pp. 3, 11, 30, 48–49 ullstein bild/Getty Images; pp. 7, 23 Hulton Archive/Getty Images; p. 13 Alinari Archives/Getty Images; p. 15 Universal Images Group/Getty Images; p. 19 Universal History Archive/Universal Images Group/Getty Images; p. 21 ©The Thoreau Society/The Walden Woods Project/The Image Works; p. 27 Underwood Archives/Archive Photos/Getty Images; pp. 32–33, 42–43, 45, 80–81 Dinodia Photos/Alamy Stock Photo; p. 39 Print Collector/Hulton Archive/Getty Images; p. 55 Culture Club/Hulton Archive/Getty Images; p. 61 Keystone/Hulton Archive/Getty Images; p. 63 © TopFoto/The Image Works; pp. 67, 77 Keystone-France/Gamma-Keystone/Getty Images; p. 69 PA Images/Alamy Stock Photo; pp. 73, 83 © AP Images; p. 87 Fox Photos/Hulton Archive/Getty Images; p. 91 Dinodia Photos/Hulton Archive/Getty Images; pp. 96–97 AFP/Getty Images; p. 99 Margaret Bourke-White/The LIFE Picture Collection/Getty Images; pp. 100–101 Mondadori Portfolio/Getty Images; interior pages borders, pp. 6–7 background Eky Studio/Shutterstock.com.

CONTENTS

INTRODUCTION

I n early March 1930, the British viceroy in India, Lord Irwin, received a very unusual letter. But, then, it was written by a very unusual man. Mohandas Karamchand Gandhi, a sixty-year-old spiritual and political leader known to his followers as Mahatma, wrote of his plans to break the British law that controlled the collection and sale of salt in India, and how the salt tax placed a particularly harsh burden on India's poor. Gandhi explained that peasant farmers used more salt than the rich because they perspired more while working in the fields under the scorching tropical sun of India.

In response to the tax, Gandhi proposed to mount a campaign of "organized nonviolence," adding in his letter to the viceroy that "this nonviolence will be expressed through civil disobedience. My ambition is no less than to … make [the British people] see the wrong they have done to India."

"If you cannot see your way to deal with these evils," continued Gandhi, "and if my letter makes no appeal to your heart, on the eleventh day of this month I shall proceed with [some] co-workers, to disregard the

Gandhi and Indian nationalist Sarojini Naidu lead peaceful
protesters during the Salt March in 1930.

provisions of the Salt Laws. It is, I know, open to you to frustrate my design by arresting me. [In that event,] I hope that there will be tens of thousands ready, in a disciplined manner, to take up the work after me."[1]

Through various news sources, word of the Mahatma's plans spread, and reporters and photographers throughout the British Empire and around the world waited and watched to see what would happen next. True to his announced plan, on March 12, Gandhi and seventy-eight of his followers left a small village, marching, as Gandhi said, "in the name of God." Their destination was Dandi, a town on the shores of the Arabian Sea. Their intended crime: to protest and break the law prohibiting the personal harvesting of salt.

The nonviolent protesters walked about 11 to 15 miles (18 to 24 kilometers) each day for twenty-four days. There was a horse available for Gandhi to ride, but he chose to walk, with only the aid of a bamboo walking stick. Some of his followers, however, took advantage of bull-drawn carts along the way.

Each day the number of followers grew as the marchers passed through village after village along the route. In a number of places, village leaders pledged to leave their jobs working for the British government as a way of joining the protest against foreign rule.

There were several thousand marchers with Gandhi when he reached the western coast of India on April 5. Camp was made and prayers were said all through the night. In the morning, after a ritual purification bath in the sea, the Mahatma walked to a place where salt lay piled on the shore and simply scooped some up.

The moment might have seemed almost anticlimactic at first. No arrests were made that day. The fuse had been lighted, however, and an observer noted, "the country simply exploded in utterly nonviolent disobedience of British law."[2]

Over the following days and weeks, with illegal acts of collecting and selling salt taking place across the land, the authorities began to respond. Soon many of the protesters were hauled off to increasingly overflowing jails. Jawaharlal Nehru, president of the Indian National Congress party and a colleague of Gandhi's, was arrested and sent to jail, as was the mayor of Calcutta. In the city of Patna, mounted police blocked a road as a crowd of Indians pressed toward a salt depot. The marchers refused to leave as ordered, and instead many lay down on the ground. The police finally resorted to carrying as many of the protesters as they could off to jail in trucks.

Then, during the night of May 4, Gandhi himself was arrested. A British officer accompanied by several dozen heavily armed policemen arrived at the place where Gandhi was camped, not far from where the march had ended at Dandi. Awakened by a flashlight shining in his face, the Mahatma was informed that he was under arrest per an old East India Company regulation dating back to 1827. He was taken to Yeravda prison. It was not the first time the Mahatma had been imprisoned, and it would not be the last.

1

Humble Birth in an Ancient Land

The boy who was named Mohandas Karamchand Gandhi was born October 2, 1869, in the small seaside region of Porbandar in western India. He was the youngest child in the family, born into a middle-ranking Hindu caste. This meant that the boy's family lived a relatively comfortable life in a land of extremes of wealth and poverty. His father held a position of some responsibility in the local government, which led to the family moving to Rajkot, some 100 miles (161 km) to the east, in 1876. His mother was a devout follower of Hinduism, the religion practiced by many Indians.

At the time of Mohandas's birth, India was considered, by the British at least, to be the jewel in the crown of the British Empire. For the millions of peasant farmers of India, however, life was difficult and the threats of disease and starvation were ever present. The vast majority of Indians lived and died by the teachings of the Hindu religion, though there was also a large number of Muslims in the land, many of whom were descendants of the Muslim Mughals who had ruled India before the arrival of the British.

Most of this would not have seemed very important to the youngest child of his father's fourth wife as he was growing up, for there was little in his early years to indicate that Mohandas would one day be called Mahatma,

Mohandas was the youngest child of Karamchand and Putlibai Gandhi.

which means "Great Soul." He was not a particularly strong student, and he was painfully shy. "My books and lessons were my sole companions," he would later recall.[1] He was also filled with fears of all sorts, including a fear of the dark, and as a youth, he could not fall asleep without a light.

As was the local custom, when Mohandas was thirteen, his parents arranged for their son to marry Kasturbai, a young girl from Porbandar, where Gandhi had been born. Kasturbai was also thirteen. Of being married at such a "preposterously" young age, Gandhi wrote in his autobiography that, with his oldest brother already married, the elders in his family decided that his second brother, two or three years older than Mohandas, a cousin who was a year older, and Mohandas would all be married at the same time, most likely as a cost-saving measure.

Though they would eventually develop a deeply caring relationship, in the early years of their marriage, the young couple acted as childish as they truly were. Mohandas was possessive and jealous. He demanded that Kasturbai ask his permission before going out, and then he would frequently tell her no. At times she went out anyway, and then there would be arguing and tears on her return.

Fortunately, the two lived together for only a short amount of time over the course of the first few years of their marriage. As they continued to go to school and grow up, they lived in their parents' homes. Mohand, as his family called him, remained very dedicated to his parents. When he was about sixteen years old, he helped care for his father, who was very ill. Already Gandhi was developing the temperament for nursing that would become an important part of his life of service.

As Gandhi completed high school, there were decisions to make that would impact the course his life

Mohandas Gandhi would travel to the Indian city of Bombay in 1888.

would take. He thought maybe he would become a doctor. But by then his father had died, and his older brother, Laxmidas, insisted that Mohandas go to England to study law because their father had wanted his youngest child to follow in his footsteps in local government. His mother, Putlibai, worried that if her young son left India, he would fall victim to the great temptations of the West—such as eating meat, drinking alcohol, and smoking cigarettes. It doesn't seem to have mattered what Kasturbai thought, though she and Mohand became parents when their first son, Harilal, was born in 1888.

ANCIENT RELIGIOUS BELIEFS

Hinduism, or at least some of the beliefs found within it, is one of the world's oldest religions, dating back thousands of years. It is believed to have started around the Indus Valley in the northwest part of the Indian subcontinent, in a region that is now the country of Pakistan. For several reasons, including the fact that it does not have one specific holy book and no single founder, Hinduism is sometimes considered a way of life more than a religion. It is a way of life followed by millions of people around the world and is by far the most commonly practiced religion in India.

In Hinduism, there are a multitude of gods and goddesses that symbolize the one abstract Supreme Being, or Brahman. Among the most important deities are Vishnu and Shiva. Hindus also believe in a cycle of life that includes birth, death, and rebirth (or reincarnation). This cycle is generally believed to be governed, or influenced, by karma (behavior, or cause and effect between actions and the future).

Traditionally, Hindu society is divided into a hierarchy of groups called castes, which people are born into. According to the caste system, if a person leads a good life, they *may* be rewarded by karma in the next life by being born into a higher caste. There are

(continued on page 16)

14

PL.I.　　　　　　　　　　　　　　　　　　　　　S:LIV.

A. Cortegan　　　　　　　　　　Lith. de Marlet & C.ᵉ, rue du Foulet, N.ᵉᵍ.

Shiva et sa femme Pàrvati.

S. शिव: पार्वती T. ஜிவன் பார்வதீ

**The Hindu god Shiva (*with mask, center*) is pictured here.
The Hindu pantheon includes many gods.**

(continued from page 14)

four main castes in the system, each of which is broken down into many subcastes. Below the fourth caste, the "lowest of the low," are the Untouchables.

Gandhi felt strongly that the extreme prejudice against the Untouchables among Hindus was every bit as cruel and wrong as the colonial oppression of the British in India. Gandhi called them *harijans*, or "children of God," and would devote a great deal of effort to improving their lot in life.

One way or another, the decision was made. Mohandas and Laxmidas would travel to Bombay where the younger brother would board a ship for England, a voyage that would take three weeks. Payment for the trip was made possible, in part, due to the not-at-all-voluntary sale of some of Kasturbai's jewelry.

But first Mohandas set out for Porbandar by means of bull-pulled cart and camelback to speak with an uncle about his plans. Like Mohandas's mother, his uncle feared that the young man would be badly influenced by Western practices. But, if Putlibai would allow it, the uncle would not interfere. After Gandhi made a solemn promise that he would stay away from wine and women and would not eat meat, permission was given for him to go. Leaving his family, he traveled to Bombay, where he would have to wait for calm seas before setting sail.

During this wait, he faced yet another challenge to his plans. Leaders of his caste did not feel it was proper for a young man of his background to make the proposed journey. At this point, the young Gandhi was so determined to go that he told these leaders that even should they declare him an outcaste, he was going.

And so, Gandhi left India for Southampton, England, on September 4, 1888. He was a month away from his nineteenth birthday.

2

An English Education

Having grown up in rural India, away from regular British contact, Gandhi found it difficult to learn how to use knives and forks at the dining table during the long ocean voyage. More seriously, though, he was determined to keep what he considered a most sacred vow: he refused to eat meat, although it was sometimes difficult to determine if the food on the ship was vegetarian or not. Fortunately, an Englishman on board befriended Gandhi and helped him out, but he also advised Gandhi that he would not survive long in England without eating meat.

When at last the ship arrived in Southampton, England, Gandhi traveled by train to London, which was one of the largest cities in the world at that time. After two nights in a hotel, a friend helped Gandhi find a small place to rent. During the coming weeks, as he struggled to find his way in this foreign land, the shy young man was very lonely. "At night," he would later recall, "the tears would stream down my cheeks and home memories of all sorts made sleep out of the question."[1]

At first, Gandhi tried to fit in by buying new clothes and dressing and behaving as an Englishman. He soon discovered that this could be quite expensive, and he began trying to balance fitting in with cutting expenses, as well as trying to bring his "inward and outward" lives

Gandhi in Western attire, as he would have looked after receiving his law credentials in England

into harmony. He adopted the habit of taking long, brisk walks every day. This helped to develop the strong physical constitution that would serve him well throughout his life.

He found the English and their ways very strange, as they, no doubt, did his. Finding food that he could eat without breaking his promise to his mother and others was very difficult. Under pressure from friends to give in and eat meat as the English did, Gandhi replied, "A vow is a vow. It cannot be broken."[2]

Finally, after moving several times, Gandhi found lodging in a home that turned out to be within walking distance of a vegetarian restaurant. In his autobiography, Gandhi relates, "The sight of it filled me with the same joy a child feels on getting a thing after its own heart. Before I entered I noticed books for sale under a glass window near the door. I saw among them Salt's *Plea for Vegetarianism*. This I purchased and went straight to the dining room. This was my first hearty meal since my arrival in England. God had come to my aid."[3]

GANDHI AND VEGETARIANISM

The earliest records of vegetarianism come from the same region as the beginnings of Hindu beliefs—that is, the Indian subcontinent. There, vegetarianism was based on respect or nonviolence (*ahimsa*) toward all living beings. Though Hindu sacred texts called meat "the food of the gods," other Hindu writings

Henry Salt, a British social activist whose writings on vegetarianism inspired and encouraged Gandhi

forbade it. One of the pillars of the ancient Indian leader Ashoka was that "one animal is not to be fed to another." Teachings such as this were likely the basis for the vegetarianism practiced by Gandhi's mother, Putlibai, and that her son promised to follow when he traveled to England as a young man. For her,

(continued on the next page)

(continued from the previous page)

and, later for him, it was not just a matter of diet; it was part of an ancient spiritual value system.

At the time of Gandhi's arrival in England, the first known vegetarian society had been founded there. It was the young man's good fortune to stumble upon a vegetarian restaurant and supportive community in West Kensington in London. Here he also became acquainted with Henry Salt's book *Plea for Vegetarianism*.

"I read Salt's book cover to cover," he would write, "and was very much impressed by it. I [now] blessed the day on which I had taken the vow before my mother. I had all along abstained from meat in the interests of truth and the vow I had taken, but had wished at the same time that every Indian should be a meat-eater, and had looked forward to being one myself freely and openly someday, and to enlisting others in the cause. The choice was now made in favor of vegetarianism, the spread of which henceforward became my mission."[4]

Both the restaurant and the book helped ensure that Gandhi's vow would be kept. More than that, they showed him that even in this strange land far from home, and even if their reasons were different than his, there were others who shared his beliefs.

Salt's book and the friends Gandhi met through his interest in vegetarianism led to his meeting and joining a circle of thinkers who spent many hours discussing such questions as, "What is the role of God in this world? Where (and how) do we find our purpose?

Henry David Thoreau wrote an essay that would become known as "Civil Disobedience" after spending a night in jail in 1846.

What responsibility do we have towards fellow inhabitants of this Earth?"[5]

Though Mohandas gradually overcame some of his fears as he matured in England, he remained shy. As a result, he developed the habit of speaking slowly and carefully. Over time, he believed this was a positive attribute, as he felt it saved him from speaking rashly or thoughtlessly. "My shyness," he would write in his autobiography, "has helped me in my discernment of truth."[6]

Gandhi's shyness also likely played a role in the voracious reader he became in England. He read English literature and religious texts of many faiths. He read American Henry David Thoreau's essay on civil disobedience and found inspiration in "The Sermon on the Mount" in the Christian Bible. And, ironically, he read the great Hindu text, the *Bhagavad Gita,* for the first time, as translated into English. This text would enlighten not only his time in England but the rest of his life.

The *Bhagavad Gita,* which means "Song of the Lord," is a 700-verse Hindu scripture that is part of a larger Hindu epic. It is written as a dialogue between Prince Arjuna and his guide and charioteer, Lord Krishna. As young Arjuna struggles to understand his duty in the face of what he sees as a righteous war between his land and another, Lord Krishna explains Arjuna's duty as a warrior and a prince. The two discuss several methods by which the prince can reach his goal of dharma, or "what is right."

In the simplest terms, the *Gita* presents an answer to the age-old question, "What are we here for?" The *Gita's* hero, Arjuna, discovers that by doing what he knows is right, without fear and without concern for reward, he can achieve holiness and oneness with God.[7]

Meanwhile, Gandhi also read the textbooks he had been told to buy for his course of study and learned what was necessary to pass examinations in Roman law and English common law. On June 10, 1891, he was "called to the bar," which means he earned his law credentials. The next day he attended a farewell party given for him by his friends in the Vegetarian Society. Then he sailed for India, after three years in the land of his country's governors.

3

An Indian Lawyer in South Africa

When Mohandas Gandhi returned to India from England in July 1891, he was greeted by his brother Laxmidas with the saddest of news. Just a short while before Gandhi's homecoming, his mother had died. With both of his parents gone, his chances of finding a position in the provincial government were greatly diminished.

Still, the young lawyer had brought home to Rajkot some British ways, such as drinking coffee and tea and dressing in the British style. Gandhi also immediately began to demand his rights as head of the household, only to find that Kasturbai, after his long absence, did the same. He would later relate that as the years passed and "the storms between them continued," he began to realize what stress he caused his wife by his authoritative attitude. At last it occurred to him that rather than exercise his rights, he could fulfill his responsibilities. As the years went by, Gandhi learned to try to win Kasturbai over by example, and he came to understand that all along, Kasturbai had been trying to win him over by love.[1]

But that would come later. For now, he went to Bombay to set up a law practice. In his first case in a small claims court, he was so nervous that he couldn't think of any questions to ask a witness. As a result, he returned the

A young Mohandas is pictured here with his older brother Laxmidas. The photograph was most likely taken shortly before Mohandas left India for England.

client's fee. Ashamed, he went home to Rajkot, where he could earn money to support his family doing work for other lawyers.

Things did not go much better closer to home. There, Gandhi had a run-in with a British official whom he had previously met in England. When Gandhi visited the office of this official, hoping only to put in a good word for Laxmidas, he was rudely told to leave. This experience, Gandhi would later write, "changed the course of my life."[2] He did not want to have to "bow down" to British authority in order to get ahead in India.

Thus, when a Muslim Indian businessman doing business in South Africa offered him work, he took it, even though it would require once again leaving Kasturbai and the two sons they now had. Gandhi sailed from Bombay on April 19, 1893. He was twenty-three years old and still trying to find his way.

The South Africa of 1893 included both British colonies and Dutch, or Boer, republics. Many Indians lived and worked there primarily in the British-controlled Cape Colony and Natal, and were mostly divided into two groups—Muslim business owners and poor Hindu laborers. Many of the laborers were indentured and hardly better off than slaves. According to the vast majority of "white" settlers in South Africa, it didn't matter if Indians were Muslim or Hindu, business owners or indentured laborers. To the Europeans, all Indians were "coloreds," or "coolies" (servants), and were looked down upon.

Shortly after his arrival, Gandhi found this out for himself. While observing a trial in an English courtroom in Durban, capital of the British colony of Natal, he was asked to remove the turban he was wearing with his English-style suit. After refusing to do so, Gandhi left the courtroom. When the incident was reported in the papers, Gandhi explained his actions by saying that while the English removed their hats as a sign of respect, in his culture, keeping his turban *on* signaled respect.

Not long after, Gandhi was on a train headed to Pretoria in the Dutch republic called the Transvaal to meet with lawyers for another case. At one point, Gandhi was bluntly ordered by a railroad official to leave the first-class section for which he had a ticket and retreat to the third-class section reserved for darker-skinned passengers. He refused and was then forced out onto a cold, deserted train station without any of his luggage in the middle of the night. As he sat in the darkness, one biographer writes, "It was not his own humiliation that infuriated him; it was the much deeper cancer of man's inhumanity to man, the persecution of whole races because of differences in skin color or belief."[3] It was also the disturbing fact that his education and professional status seemed to count for nothing. All that mattered was the color of his skin. As he continued his journey to Pretoria, fellow Indians along the way informed him that this was just how things worked in South Africa.

Just days after finally arriving in Pretoria, Gandhi spoke to fellow Indians at a meeting, asking them to ignore the differences in caste and religion among themselves in the face of common prejudice against them. More such meetings would follow, and soon Mohandas Gandhi became a prominent leader of the Indian resistance against British and Dutch racism in South Africa.

Little by little, as he worked on behalf of others, the ideal of selfless service took hold of Gandhi and led to deep changes in every aspect of his life. A little community, or *ashram* as it was called in India, grew up around

Russian writer Leo Tolstoy, with whom Gandhi corresponded about their religious beliefs and nonviolence

him in the countryside near Durban where a handful of dedicated young men and women came to live with him and share his experiments in the art of living.

Realizing that, in order to transform others, he would first have to transform himself, Gandhi purposefully set about doing exactly that. He turned to the *Bhagavad Gita* as a spiritual guide in his search for truth. At the same time, he found inspiration in several books by Christians. One was *The Kingdom of God Is Within You*, by Russian author Leo Tolstoy. In this text, Tolstoy defined the work of Christians as being willing to defy immoral laws and confront authority at great risk to themselves.[4]

Meanwhile, Gandhi attended to the business that had brought him to Pretoria, and indeed, South Africa, in the first place. The international shipping company that hired Gandhi, Dada Abdulla and Company, was owned by a wealthy Indian Muslim by that name. The case Gandhi was hired to help settle involved a complicated dispute over a considerable amount of money with another Indian Muslim, who happened to be a distant cousin of Abdulla's.

Realizing that a long court battle would do a great deal of harm to everyone involved, Gandhi found a solution that would lessen the damage by asking both parties to agree to binding arbitration, in which a neutral party would hear the case and make a decision. When Gandhi's employer was found to be in the right, Gandhi convinced him to extend generous payment terms to his opponent.

With this settlement, Gandhi felt that he had "learnt the true practice of law," by finding "the better side of human nature."[5] Whether or not this would be seen by others as the true practice of law, the settlement did increase Gandhi's standing in the eyes of the Indian

Gandhi (*center, back row*) is pictured with fellow founders of the Natal Indian Congress, dedicated to improving conditions for the Indians who lived and worked in South Africa.

community in South Africa. It also produced a self-confidence in Gandhi that would help him see future challenges and problems as opportunities for service to others.

In May 1894, with his employment coming to an end, Gandhi attended a farewell party for himself as he prepared to return to India. Having just read of a voting rights law under consideration in the Natal Legislative Assembly that would not be favorable to the Indian community, he urged his friends to form a committee or group of some sort to fight passage of the law. Gandhi's friends convinced him that they could not do battle alone, and the farewell party became a committee meeting as Gandhi was convinced to stay awhile longer.

Aware of his own youth and lack of political experience, Gandhi wrote to an Indian leader who was then in London, saying, "The responsibility taken is quite out of proportion with my ability." Concerned that others might doubt his motives, Gandhi added, "I am doing this without [pay]. So you will see that I have not taken this matter up ... to enrich myself at the expense of the Indians."[6]

With more ability than he gave himself credit for, Gandhi helped the Indian community establish the Natal Indian Congress in May 1894, inspired by the Indian National Congress, which strove to make improvements for Indians back home. As the first secretary of the Natal Indian Congress, Gandhi flooded the legislature and the public press with documentation of Indian grievances. He wrote two pamphlets aimed at spreading the word about the extent of discrimination as he and other Indians experienced it. Even a European publication in South Africa, the *Natal Mercury*, noted, "Mr. Gandhi writes with calmness and moderation. He is as impartial as anyone could expect him to be, and probably a little more so than might have been expected."[7]

In 1896, Gandhi returned briefly to India, in part to bring his family back with him to South Africa. While there he wrote another pamphlet, titled *The Grievances of the British Indians in South Africa*. With a green cover, it soon became known as "the Green Pamphlet." After a print run of ten thousand copies was distributed to newspapers and Indian leaders, a second printing was made. In sharing the facts about the injustices suffered by Indians in South Africa with those at home, Gandhi began to have a presence in his homeland.

Soon, with the Natal Indians begging him to return, Gandhi prepared to leave India again. This time, his wife, two sons, and nephew traveled with him. Upon his return to South Africa in December 1896, as he planned to continue work on behalf of the Indian community there, Gandhi came face-to-face with the brutality of prejudice once again. He and fellow passengers were initially detained on board their ship, due to exaggerated concerns about disease. When he finally walked down the ship's gangplank and onto shore, Gandhi was pelted with rocks and had his turban ripped off his head. He would write in his autobiography that he did not expect to survive. Fortunately, the wife of a local police official arrived and used her parasol to protect him until the police escorted him to a safe place where Kasturbai and the boys, who had disembarked separately from him, were waiting.

Gandhi was then forced to spend several days and nights at the police station, for his own safety and the safety of his family. He would later describe this episode as "a test" of his ability to remain nonviolent in the face of violence. Indeed, he was already beginning to gain attention for his ability to do exactly that. Soon he would ask his followers to pass this test as well.

Gandhi refused to prosecute those who had attacked him, saying that if they believed the false statements that had been made about him, it was no wonder they were enraged. This gained him, his cause, and the Indian community a measure of respect in Durban. For the rest of his life, his aim would always be to react bravely and boldly without violence in the face of violence.

> **"Man and his deed are two distinct things. 'Hate the sin and not the sinner' is a precept which, though easy enough to understand, is rarely practiced, and that is why the poison of hatred spreads in the world."[8]**

BAL GANGADHAR TILAK

Born in India in 1856, Tilak was a dedicated scholar, earning degrees in mathematics, Sanskrit, and law. After teaching in a private school, he then turned to the task of awakening the political consciousness of India, becoming widely known for his bitter criticisms of British rule.

Tilak sought to expand the reach of the nationalist movement in India by introducing Hindu religious symbols and organizing several Hindu festivals. Though that symbolism did make the nationalist movement more popular among the peasants, it also alarmed some of India's Muslims, who worried about what would happen to them in a Hindu-controlled free India. Tilak's statements also worried the British government in India, and he was charged with sedition and sent to jail in 1897. He was released after eighteen months.

When Tilak advocated a boycott of British goods in protest of other government moves in 1905, he started a movement that quickly swept the nation. The following year he called for a program of passive resistance, which he hoped would break through the hypnotic influence of British rule and prepare the people of India for the sacrifices they would need to make to gain independence.

Tilak's goal of independence from Britain, rather than reform of the Raj (as the British government in India was called), was too much for some of the more moderate nationalists, leading to a split in the Indian National Congress in 1907. Taking advantage of the divisiveness, the government again prosecuted Tilak on a charge of sedition and deported him to Burma, where he would serve a six-year prison sentence.

In 1919, Tilak changed his strategy and advised the Congress to follow a policy of "responsive cooperation" in carrying out British-suggested reforms. He died, however, before he could provide further leadership. In tributes, Gandhi called him "the Maker of Modern India." Jawaharlal Nehru, who would become independent India's first prime minister, described him as "the Father of the Indian Revolution."[9]

Meanwhile, Gandhi insisted that his family accommodate the western ways he felt would bring him and them respect. Though they objected to scratchy textiles and tight-fitting shoes, Gandhi insisted that they look "civilized." Ironically, within a short time, the domineering husband and father would again change his mind and decide that his household must simplify their way of life and abandon the hard-learned ways of the Europeans. As Gandhi struggled to find his place in between Indian, South African, and European ways, it must have been an extremely frustrating time for him and his family, which now included three sons—Harilal, Manilal, and Ramdas.

Gandhi even went so far as to insist that his wife return gifts that had been given to her as payment for his legal work. In his autobiography, he records Kasturbai making the case for keeping the gifts, saying that she "toiled for him day and night, making her weep bitter tears."[10] Another biographer writes, "She pleaded with him long and bitterly, and at last consented to his demands."[11] The gifts became part of a trust fund that would be shared within the Indian community. Gandhi would later credit Kasturbai with an endurance that was matchless.

4
The Boers, the British, and the Birth of Satyagraha

Fighting broke out between the British and the Boers in 1899. Gandhi believed that, as a subject of the British Empire, he owed the British his loyalty and service in the war, even as he protested their treatment of Indians. As he explained in his autobiography, "I felt that if I demanded rights as a British citizen, it was also my duty to participate in the defense of the British Empire."[1]

During what the British called the Boer Wars, the British and the Dutch (the Boers) fought for control of what would eventually become the nation of South Africa.

So Gandhi helped establish an Ambulance Corps made up of members of the Indian community. He believed that their bravery and sacrifice would be rewarded after the war with a change of attitude on the part of the British. Gandhi and others received medals for their service, and the British did win the war and take control of the Boer republics in South Africa; however, conditions did not improve for Indians there.

In 1901, Gandhi returned to India with his family, which now included four sons. He intended to remain in his homeland, but he had promised the Indian community in South Africa that he would come back if they needed him. In 1902, he received word that the British prime minister, Neville Chamberlain, was coming to South Africa. The Indian community hoped that if Gandhi were there, he could speak to the prime minister on their behalf.

Accompanied by his cousin's son, Maganlal Gandhi, and a few other followers, Gandhi returned to South Africa in 1903 to continue the fight for Indian rights. For the time being, Kasturbai and the rest of his family remained in India.

Gandhi's efforts to meet with the prime minister were unsuccessful. Seeing the need the community had for legal support, however, Gandhi decided to set up a law office in Johannesburg, to see what he could do to help his countrymen.

He began writing for a newspaper he helped start called the *Indian Opinion* and reported on the abusive treatment of Indians in South Africa. He also provided examples of nonviolent resistance to this sort of treatment. Each week he poured his heart and soul into the publication, explaining the principles of nonviolence that he called satyagraha (translated from Gandhi's native tongue as "holding on to truth"). The essays he wrote for the newspaper became such a part of the movement that he would write in his autobiography that "satyagraha would probably have been impossible without the *Indian Opinion*."[2]

According to Gandhi, truth could be arrived at by resisting what was morally wrong. Inspired by the teachings of the *Gita*, satyagraha also encompassed the idea of fighting without violence or retaliation. *Ahimsa*, a word often translated as "nonviolence," is the foundation of satyagraha and a key component of Buddhism as well. As Indian writer Eknath Easwaran explains, "Like the English word 'flawless,' ahimsa denotes perfection. Ahimsa is unconditional love; satyagraha is love in action."[3]

In 1904, Gandhi moved production of the *Indian Opinion* to a farm near Durban where he and his satyagrahis would labor as equals. Called the Phoenix Settlement, this was the first of two such communities, known as ashrams, that Gandhi would found in South Africa. At first the farm had only a single cottage in disrepair, a fresh-water source, and several fruit trees. Several small huts were quickly added, and Gandhi and his followers moved in. As well as being the headquarters of the *Indian Opinion*, the settlement was an experiment in simplicity, a way of living that Gandhi would follow for the rest of his life. As one author states, "The twin concepts of self-reliance and doing without had achieved a shimmering beauty in Gandhi's eyes."[4] As Gandhi settled into this life, he sent for his family to join him.

Meanwhile, news of what the British called the Zulu Rebellion reached the Phoenix Settlement. Once again,

This is the home the Gandhis lived in while at the Phoenix Settlement in South Africa.

Gandhi offered to form an Indian Ambulance Corps to assist the British cause, as he had during the Boer War.

This would be a far different experience for Gandhi, however. He would later write that the "rebellion" brought home to him the horrors of war more clearly than his experience in the Boer War. "This was no war, but a man-hunt," he said. "To hear every morning the reports of the soldiers' rifles exploding like firecrackers in innocent hamlets, was a trial." Much of the work of the ambulance corps involved providing medical attention to wounded Zulus, for, as Gandhi wrote, "I could see that but for us, the Zulu's would have been uncared for."[5]

After returning to the Phoenix Settlement in July 1906, Gandhi took the vow of *brahmacharya*, or non-possession and celibacy, to further eliminate distractions from his life and completely devote himself to service to others. He also learned of a law being debated in the Transvaal that would require Indians to register with the government or face fines, imprisonment, deportation, and other penalties. When the law was passed despite opposition, Gandhi called for the Indian community to refuse compliance with the Transvaal Asiatic Registration Act (TARA), commonly known as the Black Law. He challenged Indians to willingly accept the consequences this refusal would bring.

He made it clear that he was talking about something more than "passive resistance." What Gandhi was talking about was a new way of fighting back, and it was most certainly not "passive." A follower would later describe it with these words: "Instead of fanning hatred with hatred, and violence with violence, he argued that exploitation could be overcome by returning love for hatred and respect for contempt, in a strong, determined refusal to yield to injustice."[6]

Throughout his career as a leader of nonviolence, Gandhi would appeal to the common sense and morality of the opponent as well as the protester. When asked what he would do if nonviolence was met with violence, he replied, "I hope God will give me the courage and the sense to forgive them [the opponents]. I have no anger against them. I am only sorry for their ignorance and narrowness."[7]

Because Gandhi insisted that satyagraha was conducted in the open, with advance notice given for every action, he contacted the head of the Transvaal government, Jan Smuts, informing him of his and others' plans to resist the Black Law. When the registration deadline passed on November 30, 1907, only a little more than 500 Indians in the Transvaal had complied and registered. More than 12,000 had not.

For his role in the resistance, Mohandas Gandhi was sent to prison, along with about 150 other violators of the law. When Gandhi was sentenced to two months in a Johannesburg prison, he was given the option of paying a fine instead. Of course, Gandhi refused to pay the fine. At first, his greatest fear was that not enough of his followers would also be arrested to keep the momentum of the protest going. But soon he was joined by 150 additional satyagrahi prisoners.

Biographer Yogesh Chadha states, "There were many things about prison life that annoyed and disturbed Gandhi—the food, overcrowding, and poor ventilation—but on the whole he found it quite satisfactory, because there were few distractions and he had ample leisure for reading."[8]

In this drawing, Gandhi is shown working during one of his stays in a South African prison.

Soon, Gandhi received word that General Smuts was offering terms in an effort to end the protest. When Smuts claimed to agree with an amendment to the offer that Gandhi and his followers requested, Gandhi accepted the offer and was released from prison. At a meeting later that night, when some of those gathered voiced fear that Smuts was not to be trusted, Gandhi replied, "A Satyagrahi is never afraid of trusting the opponent. Even if the opponent plays him false twenty times, the Satyagrahi is ready to trust him the twenty-first time, for an implicit trust in human nature is the very essence of his creed."[9]

In a show of good faith, Gandhi insisted on being the first of the protesters to register under the settlement that had been reached. On his way to register, Gandhi was severely beaten by members of the Indian community, former supporters who could not accept the settlement. This experience foreshadowed later events in India, when Gandhi would be criticized for both going too far, and not far enough.

While Gandhi was recovering from the attack, the agreement was indeed found to be a ruse on the part of General Smuts. The voluntary registration of Indians was being accepted, but Smuts would not honor his pledge to repeal the Black Law.

Gandhi calmly considered the satyagrahi's next move. He informed Smuts that without the repeal of the Black Law, the Indians who had voluntarily registered would burn their certificates. On August 16, 1908, Gandhi and a large crowd of supporters burned their registration cards in a sacrificial bonfire that was compared by at least one newspaper to the Boston Tea Party.

Two months later, Gandhi was arrested when he was unable to show his (burned) registration card and sentenced to two months' hard labor. His hard labor included digging pits and breaking large stones, which he performed without complaint, as he accepted the opportunity to suffer for the cause he believed in.

While being held in Volksrust jail, Gandhi learned that Kasturbai was very ill back at the Phoenix Settlement. He wrote to her, saying, "I love you so dearly that even if you are dead, you will be alive to me. Your soul is deathless." When he was released, he received a call from the doctor caring for Kasturbai in Durban, asking if it was okay for her to have beef tea as a way to build her strength. Gandhi returned quickly to Durban to see if this was what his wife, a devout Hindu who never ate meat in any form, truly wanted and needed. The doctor insisted that if she was to remain under his care, he would have to be able to give her what he felt she needed.

But Kasturbai was adamant, saying that "she would far rather die that pollute [her] body with [beef]." Gandhi removed his wife from that doctor's care, made the journey home to Phoenix Settlement with her, and cared for her there himself. In a short amount of time, Kasturbai was fully recovered.[10]

Meanwhile, the unification of the former South African Dutch colonies with those of the British was being discussed. Gandhi went to London as a representative of the Indian community. At this point, he believed himself to be a loyal and proud member of the British Empire with all the rights that should entail. He was saddened to find that the government in England did not seem to feel the same.

His spirits were lifted, however, by re-reading Leo Tolstoy's *The Kingdom of God Is Within You*. Through this book, Gandhi came to believe that the core of the

Christian faith and the Hindu teaching of ahimsa were very similar. He was also encouraged by Tolstoy's essay titled "A Letter to a Hindu." He wrote to Tolstoy from London in October 1909, discussing the struggle of the Indian community in South Africa. In reply, Tolstoy remarked that Gandhi's letter had given him great pleasure and that he prayed that God would help Gandhi and his coworkers.

Gandhi then sent Tolstoy a copy of a recently published biography of himself, hoping that Tolstoy would share the book and spread the word about satyagraha, saying, "If it succeeds, it will be not only a triumph of religion, love and truth over irreligion, hatred, and falsehood, but it is highly likely to serve as an example to the millions in India and to people in other parts of the world, who may be downtrodden and will certainly go a great way towards breaking up the party of violence, at least in India."[11]

A moment of rest for Gandhi and others at Tolstoy Farm, one of
several ashrams Gandhi established during his life of service.

More and more, it seemed, Gandhi was considering the work that waited for him in India. On the journey from England back to South Africa in 1909, Gandhi wrote *Hind Swaraj*, which means "Indian Home Rule." Themes that would be repeated later in his efforts on behalf of Indian freedom were expressed clearly in this pamphlet. The British, he wrote, got what they wanted from India because Indians liked the products England offered. For Gandhi, home rule was about much more than forcing the English to free India. He argued that Indians needed to change their ways before they would be ready to govern themselves, for freedom without morality was of little interest to Gandhi. And the morality and principles he was most interested in included cooperation between Hindus, Muslims, and other religions practiced in India, the elimination of "untouchability" from Indian society, and the revival of Indian cottage industries—specifically the spinning of cotton—which he believed would return Indians to a more self-reliant way of life and end dependence on British goods.

Upon his return to South Africa, Gandhi established a new community, Tolstoy Farm, in honor of the Russian writer. Many of the people in this community were family members of imprisoned satyagrahis, uprooted by the protests. Gifts from supporters in South Africa and India provided funds, and a wealthy friend donated a 1,100-acre (445-hectare) farm outside of Johannesburg.

As an additional insult, the Transvaal government in South Africa passed a series of immigration laws and ruled that only Christian marriages were legal. This had the effect of bringing Indian women, including Kasturbai, into the resistance movement. On September 15, 1913, a

TOLSTOY AND GANDHI

In 1908, Gandhi read "A Letter to a Hindu," written by the Russian author of the epic novel *War and Peace*. Tolstoy had also written a great deal about nonresistance, and "A Letter to a Hindu" was his reply to an Indian revolutionary who had challenged Tolstoy's philosophy. Gandhi was so impressed by it that he sought Tolstoy's permission to publish the letter in South Africa. Tolstoy agreed to Gandhi's request and also consented to having his writings translated into various Indian dialects.

Both Gandhi and Tolstoy had widely read the works of religious and philosophical thinkers, and both were staunch advocates of human brotherhood and the unity of all creation. Tolstoy often wrote that brotherhood extends to the lowest and the poorest of creation. Gandhi believed in that as well. For Tolstoy, religion encompasses one's relation with the whole universe, of which man constitutes only a part. Religion is a relationship man sets up between himself and the infinite universe. In the same vein Gandhi stated, "I am a part and parcel of the whole and I cannot find God apart from the rest of humanity."[12]

In Tolstoy's last letter to Gandhi, he wrote,

"The more I live—and especially now that I am approaching death, the more I feel inclined to express to others the feelings which so strongly

(continued on the next page)

51

(continued from the previous page)

move my being. That is, what one calls nonresistance, is in reality nothing else but the discipline of love undeformed by false interpretation. That love is the supreme and unique law of human life which everyone feels in the depth of one's soul. That law of love has been promulgated by all the philosophies—Indian, Chinese, Hebrew, Greek and Roman. I think that it had been most clearly expressed by Christ. Christ knew, just as all reasonable human beings must know, that the employment of violence is incompatible with love, which is the fundamental law of life. He knew that once violence is admitted—it doesn't matter in even a single case—the law of love is thereby rendered futile."[13]

Gandhi couldn't have said it better himself.

group of Indians crossed the border from Natal into the Transvaal, in violation of the new immigration law. The members of the group were arrested and sentenced to hard labor.

This was followed by a march of more than two thousand men, women, and children across the border from Natal into the Transvaal and toward Tolstoy Farm. Along the way, Gandhi and several other leaders of the march were jailed and sentenced to hard labor.

Meanwhile, a group of women from Tolstoy Farm convinced several thousand indentured Indian miners to go on strike. The women were arrested and sentenced to hard labor while the miners were herded onto trains and taken back to the mines. When they refused to go back to work, they were beaten. This only served to ignite further resistance.

One result of the protests and the response of the authorities in the Union of South Africa was an increase in worldwide attention to conditions there, and a commission was set up to investigate the Indians' grievances. Gandhi was released from prison.

Slowly but surely, over the next few years, some of the concerns of the Indians in South Africa were addressed. On January 21, 1914, Gandhi and Smuts reached another agreement, and in the next several months, more of the offensive laws were repealed. Gandhi at last determined that the time had come for him to return to India.

> **"It was my fate to be the protagonist of a man for whom even then I had the highest respect."[14] – General Jan Smuts, on Gandhi**

Years later, General Smuts would admit that Gandhi had won the "battle" between them "by his courage, by his determination, by his refusal to take unfair advantage, [and] especially by his endless capacity to 'stick it out,' without yielding and without retaliation."[15]

Gandhi sailed from South Africa for the final time on July 18, 1914, sailing first to London, and then finally, home to India. Shortly before departing, he gave General Smuts a pair of sandals that he had made in prison.

5

Great Soul

When Gandhi returned to India in 1915, World War I had begun and Indians were expected to support the British cause. As he had done in South Africa, Gandhi once again championed Indian participation in the war effort, believing it would strengthen the argument for treating Indians as equals when the war was won.

Though most of his work to that point had been outside of his homeland, Gandhi's name was already familiar to leaders in the Indian National Congress and the nationalist movement. However, since he had been gone for so many years, one of his mentors suggested that the newly returned Gandhi take some time to get reacquainted with India. Gandhi took this advice to heart and made very few public statements during the first year after his return. Instead, he spent time traveling—particularly among the poor—observing, and writing.

Among the observations that Gandhi made was noting that the "westernization" of India had caused many problems in the land, calling it "the true badge of slavery of the Indian people." At the same time, he believed, to a certain extent, that "India's shackles were self-made."[1]

Indian soldiers fought for the British, and against the German army, during World War I.

"No people exists that would not think itself happier under its own bad government than it might really be under the good governance of an alien power."[2]

Gandhi believed that one of the best ways for Indians to break the chains of control that England held over them was with cottage industries such as hand-spinning and handloom weaving. The weaving and wearing of handmade Indian cloth, called *khadi*, would provide employment for the poor and self-sufficiency for India. For Gandhi and his followers, the simple spinning wheel, or *charkha*, became a symbol of independence and khadi became the peoples' uniform.

It was during these early years after his return to India that Mohandas Gandhi became widely referred to as Mahatma, a title meaning "Great Soul." Rabindranath Tagore, a Nobel Prize–winning poet of India, referred to Gandhi as a "Great Soul in peasant's garb," and the name became synonymous with Gandhi and his work forever after. From vast crowds of peasants the cry of "Mahatmaji" and "Gandhiji" arose over and over again. (The suffix "ji" shows respectful affection.) As years passed, he was also known as "Bapu," or papa.

As he had in South Africa, Gandhi founded a community of followers shortly after his return to India. In 1917, with the help of some friends and businessmen, he moved the Satyagraha Ashram, as this new community was known, to a permanent location across the Sabarmati River from Ahmedabad. Ashramites vowed to do all the work on the property and to strive to live simply, nonviolently, and self-sufficiently.

ISLAM IN INDIA

The religion of Islam was founded in the year 610 when the prophet Muhammad is said to have received a revelation from the angel Gabriel. Muhammad shared his message with his followers, who helped him spread the teachings of Islam throughout the Arabian Peninsula and, from there, to other parts of the world.

When Muslims—people who practice Islam—arrived in India, they built mosques, spread their religion, and established trade. The Mughal dynasty, led by Muslims from central Asia, ruled much of northern India from the early sixteenth to the mid-eighteenth century. The Mughals were known as effective rulers and able administrators.

Over many centuries, Islam coexisted in various parts of the Indian subcontinent with Hinduism, Jainism, and Buddhism. That coexistence became more challenging after World War I, when differing opinions arose about how a free India would be governed. As time passed, some Muslim leaders, notably Muhammad Ali Jinnah, became determined to create a separate nation from the part of India where Muslims were in the majority. Others continued to work with Gandhi and the Indian National Congress toward a united India. In 1947, due in part to Jinnah's efforts, the nation of Pakistan was created as an independent Muslim state. However, Islam remains the second-most practiced religion after Hinduism in India today.

In 1916, Gandhi attended the Lucknow session of the Indian National Congress. A group of nationalist leaders pushed through a resolution asking the British to declare their "aim and intention to confer self-government on India at an early date." Also during this session, Hindu leaders of the Congress found common ground with leaders of another nationalist organization in India, the All-India Muslim League. In what became known as the Lucknow Pact, the Muslim League joined the Indian National Congress in proposing greater self-government for India.

In response to the Lucknow Pact, the viceroy suggested that the British parliament demonstrate its "good faith"—especially in light of the Indian role in fighting the Great War—through a number of public actions, including giving awards and other honors to Indian soldiers. In August 1917, the secretary of state for India, Edwin Montagu, announced in London the British aim of including more Indians in governing institutions "with a view to progressive realization of responsible government in India." [3]

With a great many of the British soldiers previously stationed in India now fighting in the battlefields of World War I, there was heightened concern about any activities that might threaten the Raj, or British rule in India. To alleviate these concerns, the Defense of India Act of 1915 was passed, allowing the government to arrest and imprison "politically dangerous dissidents" without due process. It was under the Defense of India Act that a number of key Muslim League and Congress leaders were arrested in 1916 and 1917.

This was the setting in which Gandhi resumed his service work in 1917 in the Champaran district of Bihar, near the northern border of India. A poor farmer had sought the Mahatma out and explained the tenant system under which he and others had struggled for many years. First they were forced into planting indigo, harvested for use as a textile dye, on a portion of their land. Then they were required to sell it at below-market prices to British landowners.

As was his custom, Gandhi first tried to understand all sides of the situation and did not hide the purpose of his visit to Bihar. When British authorities realized that the Mahatma was there, and what he was there for, they ordered him to leave at once. He refused. Under pressure from the British viceroy, who was anxious to maintain peace in India while England was engaged in war, the provincial government eventually cancelled the order requiring Gandhi to leave and later agreed to study the situation. In time, the tenant farmers received repayment of at least some of what they were owed by the landlords.

In discussing his experience at Champaran, Gandhi would later say, "What I did was a very ordinary thing. I declared that the British could not order me around in my own country." He would also say that working with the peasants there had brought him "face-to-face with God, ahimsa, and Truth."[4]

Soon afterward, he urged mill workers in Ahmedabad to go on strike after taking a pledge that they would not go back to work until their demands were met and that they would not resort to violence. Every day, Gandhi met the strikers under a spreading acacia tree near the Sabarmati River. He called for "discipline, determination, and the acceptance of suffering."[5]

The mill owners did not seem willing to listen to the workers, and as time wore on, fewer workers gathered under the acacia tree each morning. Fearing that the strikers would give in, Gandhi challenged them, saying that if the peaceful strike did not continue until a reasonable settlement was reached, he would begin a hunger strike. In his autobiography, Gandhi wrote that the workers were "thunderstruck" by this statement, saying, "Not you but we shall fast. Please forgive us for our lapse, we shall now remain faithful to our pledge to the end."[6]

Gandhi did fast for three days and then instructed the workers to go to the mill owners with a request for a wage increase. The mill owners agreed, and the strike finally came to an end. Both the fast and the careful determination of the facts surrounding the injustice he was investigating would reappear as strategies in additional satyagraha campaigns.

Gandhi also led a satyagraha in Kaira, a rural area of Gujarat where land-owning farmers were protesting increased taxes. Although the farmers' cause received attention from Gandhi's involvement, the satyagraha itself, which consisted of the farmers' collective decision to withhold payment of taxes, was not immediately successful, as the British authorities refused to back down. It was during this satyagraha, however, that Gandhi formed a lifelong bond with Sardar Vallabhbhai Patel, who had organized the farmers and who would go on to play a leadership role in the Indian independence movement along with Gandhi. Champaran, Kaira, and Ahmedabad were important milestones in the history of Gandhi's new methods of social protest in India.

As the Great War at last came to a bitter end, Gandhi and other Indian leaders awaited an announcement of changes in Britain's plans for India. Instead, a committee chaired by a British judge named Sidney Rowlatt presented

Sidney Rowlatt, the British judge who ordered what became known as the Rowlatt Acts, sparking widespread protests in India

a report in July 1918 that identified three regions in India where they felt that there was heightened risk of revolutionary activities: Bengal, Bombay, and the Punjab. To minimize these risks, the committee recommended that the government continue to use the emergency powers it had claimed in wartime, including the ability to arrest and detain suspects without trial. These recommendations would be enforced by passage of the Rowlatt Acts in March 1919.

Clearly, though the war was over, Britain was determined to keep as tight a hold as ever on India.

6

The Rowlatt Protests and Massacre at Amritsar

During wartime, those who criticized the British government were subject to arrest on charges of sedition. As the Rowlatt Committee reported its findings, many Indian nationalists were in prison. This included the founders of two separate home rule leagues: Bal Gangadhar Tilak, an outspoken Indian nationalist, and

British officers in Amritsar at the site of peaceful protests that turned violent and were followed by the massacre of peaceful protesters in Jallianwala Bagh.

Annie Besant, an Irish-born supporter of Indian rights, as well as key Indian Muslim leaders.

Now, with the passage of the Rowlatt Acts, Mahatma Gandhi moved to the forefront of the nationalist movement. He called on Indians across the country to observe a general *hartal* (a closing down of all places of business and work) and a day of fasting and prayer. Gandhi believed that without the participation of Indian workers, all economic activity in the country would come to a halt. The great masses of India would demonstrate to Britain and the world the power of nonviolent protest.

The nonviolent hartal began in Delhi on March 30. Nine protesters were killed when authorities opened fire on them. In Bombay, where Gandhi had proposed to begin the hartal on April 6, six hundred men and women signed the satyagraha pledge. Gandhi spoke to a huge gathering, reminding the people that though the government might react with violence, satyagraha required that the protesters respond with ahimsa, or loving nonviolence.

Gandhi described the first day of the general strike as "a most wonderful spectacle." However, in what he termed "a Himalayan miscalculation" of India's understanding of satyagraha, the protests were quickly marred by arson, assaults on Englishmen, and other acts of violence in various parts of India. On April 18, 1919, Gandhi called for an end to the campaign, dismayed by the lack of discipline among the crowds of protesters.

In the meantime, unbeknownst to Gandhi and most of India at the time, an act of massive violence had occurred in the Punjab province. There, in the city of Amritsar, peaceful hartals had taken place on March 30 and April 6. Several days later, however, after two Congress party leaders were arrested, soldiers fired on a large crowd as the people tried to push their way through to where the leaders were being held. With dead and wounded in the street, mayhem broke out throughout the city. A British schoolteacher was brutally attacked by Indian protesters and left for dead.

Then, on Sunday April 13, 1919, a mass meeting of Indians took place in a walled courtyard known as Jallianwala Bagh. When British Brigadier General Dyer, the officer in charge of the area, learned of this, he decided to "inflict punishment" on those who defied his orders forbidding all public meetings, whether the offenders knew of those orders or not.

Meanwhile, in Jallianwala Bagh, nonviolent Indian protesters passed two resolutions: one calling for a repeal of the Rowlatt Acts, and one expressing sympathy for the loss of life in the violence that had taken place three days earlier. As Gandhi biographer Yogesh Chadha relates: "Suddenly the sound of heavy boots was heard. As soon as General Dyer entered [Jallianwala Bagh] he ordered [his troops] to fire into the crowd until all their ammunition was exhausted. For ten minutes, the riflemen fired accurately and deliberately, carefully selecting their targets. In all, 1,650 rounds were fired, killing 379 persons and wounding 1,137.[1]

Afterward, with no care offered to the wounded Indians, Dyer declared martial law, allowing no word of the massacre out of the city. He then issued a series of orders that were meant to further bully and humiliate the people of Amritsar. Indians who wished to pass down the street where the schoolteacher had been attacked were required to crawl, or face punishment by flogging. Public floggings were also ordered for offenses like disregarding a curfew order, refusing to properly greet British officers, and tearing down official proclamations. Six of the largest boys at a high school were flogged simply because they were big schoolboys.[2]

It's not hard to imagine that these events became a turning point in Indian resistance against the British. For his part, Gandhi could now see more clearly what British rule meant for India and could no longer consider himself a loyal member of the empire. Though he had already ended satyagraha by the time he learned of the massacre at Amritsar, he was not about to cease his efforts to bring the British Raj to an end.

The Indian National Congress held its annual session at Amritsar that year. Prominent Congress leader Jawaharlal Nehru would refer to this as "the first Gandhi Congress" and observed that, despite the halt of the satyagraha campaign, "the majority of the delegates and even more so the crowds outside, looked to Gandhi for leadership."[3]

Meanwhile, a new Government of India Act offered some reforms. Some departments in the Indian government were transferred from British control to the provinces of India. The provinces themselves would now be administered under a new system, with control of areas such as education, agriculture, and infrastructure development. These so-called "Montagu-Chelmsford" reforms offered Indians an opportunity to exercise some local power, but they were considered too little, too late, by many of the Indian leaders.

With the post–World War I breakup of the Turkish Empire (the Turks having sided with Germany in the war), Gandhi sought unity between the Hindu and Muslim parts of India against the British. He proposed a strategy called "noncooperation" that would include the leadership of both religious groups. As Gandhi saw it, with

Jawaharlal Nehru would become the first prime minister of India in 1947.

noncooperation on the part of Indians, the machinery of the Raj would gradually grind to a halt.

After several delays to provide the British an opportunity to deliver on past promises, Gandhi began his campaign of noncooperation in 1920. Indians followed his lead in returning British awards and honors and boycotting British goods. In addition, Gandhi reorganized the Congress, transforming it into a mass movement and opening its membership to even the poorest Indians. At the Nagpur Congress session of 1920, Gandhi spoke optimistically of independence within a year if the movement remained nonviolent. But the next year passed without any significant movement toward independence. Gandhi answered questions about this by saying that for him, *swaraj*, or independence, included personal and national self-control, and until Indians fully understood that, he did not feel political independence would come.

On March 10, 1922, the British police arrested Gandhi and charged him with sedition because of statements he'd made in *Young India*, the weekly journal that Gandhi published. A trial was held in Ahmedebad, not far from Satyagraha Ashram. Serving as his own lawyer, Gandhi pleaded guilty, saying, "I knew that I was playing with fire, but I had to make my choice. I had either to submit to a system which I considered had done irreparable harm to my country, or incur the risk of the mad fury of my people bursting forth. I am here, therefore, to invite and cheerfully submit to the highest penalty that can be inflicted upon me." In a statement he read in court, Gandhi traced his journey from his first encounters with British authority in South Africa to recent events wherein he concluded that "the British connection had made India

HABITUAL

11

Protesters arrested by the Raj, Poona, India, May 1930

more helpless than ever she was before, economically and politically."[4]

When Gandhi finished, the judge sentenced him to six years in prison, following a precedent set previously in the sentencing of the Indian nationalist Tilak. Gandhi regarded this sentence as "a privilege and an honor." Before leaving the courtroom, the British judge bowed to the loincloth-clad Mahatma, who returned the gesture. As biographer Chadha notes, it was not the last time Gandhi was sent to prison, but it was the last time the British authorities put him on trial.[5]

> **"Select your purpose, and then use self-less means to attain your goal. Do not resort to violence even if it seems at first to promise success. Use the means of love and respect even if the result seems far off or uncertain. Then throw your heart and soul into the campaign, counting no price too high for working for the welfare of those around you, and every reverse, every defeat, will send you deeper into your own deepest resources. Violence can never bring an end to violence; all it can do is provoke more violence."[6]**

Gandhi soon found himself in Yeravda jail, a place he would spend enough time in to sometimes refer to it as home. Though it was not a particularly pleasant place, Gandhi found reasons to almost enjoy his time there. In prison, he had time to meditate and pray, to read, and to write. He always kept his charkha at hand and had time for daily spinning.

KHADI

Khadi is the ancient craft of hand spinning and hand weaving as practiced in India for thousands of years. It is also the name for the cloth, most often spun from coarse cotton, that is produced. Archaeologists have found evidence that the Indus River Valley civilization had a well-developed tradition of cloth making as far back as 2800 BCE.

During his lifetime, Mahatma Gandhi saw the potential of reintroducing khadi production as a tool for a self-reliant, independent India. "The spinning wheel represents to me the hope of the masses," he claimed. "The masses lost their freedom, such as it was, with the loss of the *charkha* [spinning wheel]." He understood that more than the production and sale of this handwoven fabric was at stake. He convinced his followers that independence and khadi were synonymous. "If we have the 'khadi spirit' in us," he told India, "We will surround ourselves with simplicity in every walk of life. The 'khadi spirit' means patience. As spinners and weavers toil at their trade, even so must we have patience while we are spinning 'the thread of swaraj.'"[7]

Introduced for the purpose of boycotting foreign goods, khadi became a national movement under Gandhi. The All India Spinners Association was launched with the intention of producing and selling khadi in 1925. After independence and Gandhi's death, the khadi movement continued. Today, the

(continued on the next page)

(continued from the previous page)

Khadi and Village Industries Commission is responsible for the planning, promotion, organization, and implementation of programs for the development of khadi and other village industries in rural areas of India. India now celebrates Khadi Day on September 19.

On January 12, 1924, Gandhi was taken from Yeravda to the hospital in Poona where he was operated on for appendicitis. His recovery was slowed when an abscess developed. The government decided to release the Mahatma rather than risk having him die a martyr's death while in their custody.

As he recovered, Gandhi learned that the Hindu-Muslim alliance he had tried to cultivate had collapsed and the noncooperation movement had stalled. The Mahatma decided to devote his attention to some of the social aspects of his interpretation of true independence: the production and wearing of khadi and the end of untouchability.

7
The March Toward Swaraj

A t its annual session in Lahore in 1929, Jawaharlal Nehru, by then president of the Indian National Congress, issued a demand for complete independence. The declaration was drafted by the Working Committee of the Congress, which included Gandhi, Nehru, and Patel. Gandhi subsequently led an expanded movement of civil disobedience, culminating in 1930 with

Sarojini Naidu leads protesters in the Dharasana Satyagraha in protest of the Salt Laws, May 1930.

his march to the sea and the salt satyagraha that followed, in which thousands of Indians defied the tax on salt by gathering and selling their own.

After Gandhi was arrested for his part in breaking the law, it fell to poet and nationalist leader Sarojini Naidu to lead some two thousand satyagrahis to the Dharasana Saltworks, north of Bombay. There, the protesters marched toward the salt flats being guarded by Indian policemen and British officers. The marchers ignored orders to disperse, continuing to walk slowly and silently forward. As a reporter who was on the scene later described, "At a word of command, scores of native policemen rushed upon the marchers and rained blows on their heads with their steel-shod lathis [a long stick used as a weapon]. Not one of the marchers even raised an arm to fend off blows. They went down like ten-pins." The reporter, Webb Miller, would later say, "In eighteen years of reporting in twenty-two countries, during which I have witnessed innumerable civil disturbances, riots, street-fights, and rebellions, I have never witnessed such harrowing scenes as Dharasana." [1]

Gandhi's son Manilal was among those arrested at Dharasana. Congress leader Vallabhbhai Patel, who visited the area soon afterward, said, "All hope of reconciling India with the British Empire is lost forever. I can understand any government taking people into custody and punishing them for breaches of the law, but I cannot understand how any government that calls itself civilized can deal as savagely and brutally with nonviolent, unresisting [protesters] as the British have this morning." [2]

Many of the Indian leaders arrested during the salt protests, including Gandhi, were released from jail in early 1931. Gandhi and the viceroy, Lord Irwin, began a series

JAWAHARLAL NEHRU

Jawaharlal Nehru was born into a wealthy and powerful Hindu family in Allahabad, India, on November 14, 1889. Tutored at home until the age of fifteen, Nehru then, like Gandhi and many of the other Indian nationalists, went to England for further education. After studying law in London, he returned to India at the age of twenty-two, where he practiced law with his father, Motilal Nehru.

In 1916, Nehru entered an arranged marriage with Kamala Kaul. The following year, a daughter named Indira was born. (Indira would grow up to follow in her father's footsteps one day, known to the world as Indira Gandhi, not related to the Mahatma.)

Thoroughly westernized when he returned to India, the young Nehru joined other nationalists in opposing the British Raj. Though he never came to agree completely with the Mahatma, he greatly respected and revered Gandhi, and soon became his trusted follower. During the noncooperation movement of 1920–1922, Nehru was imprisoned for his part in the protests. Over the course of the next two and a half decades, Nehru spent a total of nine years in jail.

On August 15, 1947, India finally gained its independence, and Nehru became the nation's first prime minister. Amid the celebration, there was also considerable turmoil as independence was

(continued on the next page)

(continued from the previous page)

accompanied by partition into the separate nations of Pakistan and India.

Throughout his seventeen-year leadership, Nehru advocated democratic socialism and secularism and encouraged India's industrialization. He also promoted advancements through higher learning and instituted various social reforms such as free public education and meals for Indian children, legal rights for women, and laws to prohibit discrimination based on caste.

Nehru requested foreign aid after China invaded India's northern border in 1962. The conflict, known as the Sino-Indian War, had a profound effect on Nehru's health, resulting in a severe stroke in January of 1964 and his death a few months later.

of talks in February that led to a settlement that became known as the Irwin-Gandhi Pact. Signed on March 5, 1931, the agreement called for an end to the civil disobedience campaign in advance of a second Round Table Conference that would be held in London in the fall of 1931 and which Gandhi would attend. (A first conference had been held in 1930 without any representation from the Congress.) The agreement also allowed Indians living near the coast to gather salt for their own use.

In a letter to King George V, the viceroy described Gandhi with these words:

> *"I think that most people meeting him would be conscious of a very powerful personality, and this, independent of physical endowment, which indeed*

Mohandas and Kasturbai Gandhi's second son, Manilal

is unfavorable. Small, wizened, rather emaciated, no front teeth, it is a personality very poorly adorned with the world's trimmings. And yet you cannot help feeling the force of character behind the sharp little eyes and the immensely active and acutely working mind."[3]

Gandhi arrived in London in mid-September 1931 for the conference. As author Arthur Herman relates, "For the next two and a half months, his bald head, naked legs, and what the press called 'his loincloth and shawl,' would become a familiar sight in the streets of London."[4] Since the publicity of the salt march and subsequent satyagraha campaigns, the Mahatma was a well-known figure around the world and certainly in England.

> **When someone asked Gandhi why he always traveled third-class, among the poor, he answered simply, "Because there is no fourth."**[5]

Making clear what he hoped to gain from the conference, Gandhi appealed "to the conscience of the world" in a radio broadcast to "come to the rescue of a people dying to regain [their] liberty."[6] He would leave England without seeing his goals met, but it would be a misstatement to say that the trip was not worthwhile.

Part of the reason Gandhi's goals would not be met was due to the efforts of a British statesman by the name of Winston Churchill. As strongly as Gandhi demanded freedom for India, Churchill would hold out against it. Churchill thought the negotiations between the viceroy and Gandhi were nothing but a "spectacle" and a "most injurious blow at British authority, not only in India, but throughout the globe."[7]

Another part was that though Gandhi represented the Congress, and Congress claimed to represent India, there was, in fact, another representative of India present—the Aga Khan, spokesperson for millions of Muslims in the Indian subcontinent. An inability of the various factions within India to unify—not only Hindus and Muslims, but Sikhs and other religious minorities as well as representatives of the Untouchables who wanted separate representation—doomed the Conference.

While in London, Gandhi chose to stay at a settlement house called Kingsley Hall, founded by one of Gandhi's British supporters. Visitors from all over England and around the world streamed into the house to discuss a variety of issues with the Mahatma, often while he sat spinning at his ever-present charkha. And it was from Kingsley Hall, in a working-class section of London's East End, that Gandhi walked the city's streets clad in a loincloth, interacting with the English people whose government he was opposing. A delightful story is told that on one of his early-morning walks, a young boy provided the Mahatma with a hearty laugh when he shouted, "Hey Gandhi! Where's your trousers?"[8]

Gandhi even made it a point to visit Lancashire, an economically depressed textile region hard-hit by the Indian boycott of foreign-made cloth. After listening attentively to the out-of-work British laborers, Gandhi gently explained that where England had unemployment, India experienced starvation. If they went to India, Gandhi continued, they would "find half-starved skeletons, living corpses."[9] Many of the textile workers became supporters of Gandhi that day.

While attending the Round Table Conference in 1931, Gandhi stayed at Kingsley Hall settlement house, where he could interact with the working-class people of London.

When the Round Table Conference closed without having made any significant progress, Gandhi headed home to India. He arrived in Bombay in the closing days of 1931. On January 4, 1932, he was arrested, again under Regulation XXV of 1827, which permitted him to be detained without trial, and sent to Yeravda jail. Many other nationalist leaders were also jailed throughout India, sparking widespread boycotts and other protests. In January and February, more than thirty thousand people were convicted of political offenses. In some cases, the police were ordered to fire into crowds of protesters, resulting in many casualties.

In September, Gandhi began a "fast unto death" to protest British plans for a "communal electorate," which would provide separate representation in the Indian legislatures for Untouchables. Gandhi felt strongly that this was not the way to deal with the people he called "Harijans," and that it was a way of dividing the lower classes from the main Hindu community. Ironically, some of Gandhi's most vocal opponents on this issue were some of the Untouchables themselves, who had other ideas about what was best for them.

While Gandhi fasted and negotiations between the concerned parties were held, the Mahatma's condition declined dangerously. As his blood pressure rose and he grew increasingly weak, Gandhi lay on a cot in the Yeravda prison courtyard waiting as a compromise was hammered out, cabled to London, approved by the British government, and returned to Gandhi and his followers. On September 26, 1932, Kasturbai handed her husband a glass of orange juice, and the Mahatma's fast ended. Gandhi remained at Yeravda.

But not for long. Though there were some notable changes in the treatment of Untouchables on the part of India's Hindus, Gandhi was not satisfied that there had been enough progress. On May 8, 1933, he began another fast, this time, he said, not unto death, but for a period of twenty-one days. Considering that the previous fast had left him on death's door after only six days, his followers feared the worst.

Somehow, however, he defied death to live until the twenty-one days came to an end on May 29. Released from Yeravda and very quickly imprisoned again, he began yet another fast unto death in August 1933, this time in protest of being kept from his Harijan work in prison. In extremely fragile condition, he was taken to the hospital and from there released unconditionally.

After recovering at a friend's home, having given Satyagraha Ashram to a Harijan group, Gandhi spent ten months traveling around the country, speaking and collecting for the Harijan cause. During this time the Mahatma and Kasturbai would deal with a more personal trial as well. Their son Harilal had converted to Islam in defiance of his father. Gandhi would write, "If this acceptance was from the heart, I should have no quarrel. For, I believe Islam to be as true a religion as my own."[10] But Gandhi knew of Harilal's habits of drinking and "visiting

Kasturbai Gandhi in 1942, after many years of sharing her husband's life of service

houses of ill fame," and knew that Harilal's conversion was not truthful.

Kasturbai was also very upset by her eldest son's behavior, writing to him, "What has grieved me greatly is your criticism of your father, in which you have been indulging nowadays. Your father is no doubt bearing it all so bravely, but I am an old weak woman, who finds it difficult to suffer patiently the mental torture caused by your regrettable way of life."[11]

Meanwhile, a strong showing by Congress in the communal elections of 1937 meant that Congress ministries were formed in seven Indian provinces as the wheels of the government reform process moved agonizingly slowly. This was good news for the Congress but bad news, in the long run, for India. The poor showing by the Muslim League in the election increased Muslim fears about a Congress-controlled India. Though Congress insisted that it was a secular organization for Hindus, Muslims, and others, many Muslims were not convinced. Congress continued to oppose dividing India along religious lines. Its leadership blamed the British for "divide and rule" tactics that caused Muslims to regard Hindus as a threat.

From that time on, however, Muslim leader Jinnah rejected the establishment of a united India, proclaiming what he called the Two-Nation Theory in March 1940. "Islam and Hinduism," he claimed, "are not religions in the strict sense of the word, but are, in fact, different and distinct social orders. They belong to two different civilizations which are based mainly on conflicting ideas and conceptions."[12]

By that time Great Britain was involved in the Second World War. Again, Gandhi's sympathies were with Britain, and in fact, as he and the viceroy discussed the possibility that Westminster Abbey and other great buildings in London might be destroyed by the Luftwaffe (the German air force), he was moved to tears. The leadership of Congress, meanwhile, insisted that if India was going to have to play a part in "Britain's war," it would expect some deep concessions in return.

In 1942, the Cripps Mission arrived in India, attempting to secure the Congress's cooperation in the war effort in exchange for a promise of independence as soon as the war ended. Top officials in Britain, most notably Prime Minister Winston Churchill, did not support this goal, and negotiations with the Congress in India soon broke down.

Gandhi was now seventy-two years old, and growing tired of continued negotiations and waiting for swaraj. He demanded that the British "quit India," although, in the interest of stopping the Axis powers fighting in World War II, British and Allied forces would be allowed to operate from the subcontinent for the duration of the war. Gandhi made it clear that India freed from British control would still support the Allies.

As Gandhi and the Indian National Congress considered the fine points of the "Quit India movement," the British government arrested thousands of national, provincial, and local Congress leaders. The country erupted in violent demonstrations that the large wartime British army presence in India quickly, and violently, crushed.

8
War and Disunity

In 1939, at the start of World War II, the viceroy proclaimed (without having consulted with any Indians) that India was joined with England in the war against Germany. Though Gandhi's sympathies were most certainly with England and France in their fight against Hitler, he was less inclined to wait until yet another war was over before securing Indian independence.

Meanwhile, on October 17, 1939, the viceroy issued a statement that dominion status, meaning that India would be only semi-independent from Britain, remained Britain's goal in India. Gandhi, and virtually all of India's leaders, found the statement very disappointing. Unfortunately for a united India, the Congress's refusal to work with the British at this stage left the Muslim League room to negotiate their goal of a separate Muslim state with the British Raj.

The Indian National Congress passed a "Quit India" resolution in August 1942, calling upon England to grant independence to India. Gandhi declared that he wanted "freedom immediately, this very night, if it could be had."[1] He planned to initiate a new satyagraha, but the very next day he and numerous other Congress members were arrested. This time, Gandhi was detained in the run-down palace of the Aga Khan in Poona. Kasturbai soon joined him after breaking the law by speaking to a crowd

The khadi-wrapped Mahatma prepares to meet with the British viceroy and other leaders of the Indian National Congress.

in Bombay. A week later, the Mahatma was devastated when Mahadev Desai, Gandhi's long-time secretary who'd been like a son to him, had a heart attack and died in the prison.

> **"Noncooperation with evil is as much a duty as is cooperation with good. In the past, noncooperation has been expressed in violence to the evil-doer. I am endeavoring to show to my countrymen that violent noncooperation only multiples evil, and that as evil can only be sustained by violence, withdrawal of support for evil requires complete abstention from violence."[2]**

With the arrest of their leaders and Desai's death leading to rumors of mistreatment, mobs of Indians took to the streets in violent protest despite Gandhi's teachings. Once again, the British responded with force. In England, Churchill announced that "the disturbances had been crushed." He went on to famously say that England would remain the rulers of India for a long time, adding, "I have not become the King's First Minister in order to preside over the liquidation of the British Empire."[3]

At the end of January 1943, Gandhi informed Lord Linlithgow, the current viceroy, that on February 9, he would begin a twenty-one day fast in prison. Gandhi made it clear that he was not calling this a fast unto death, for he did not want to die. Rather, he was fasting in protest of British claims that the violence that followed his and others' arrests was his fault.

THE BRITISH RAJ

The British Raj is the name commonly given to British control over India between the Revolt of 1857, when power was officially transferred from the East India Company to the British government, and Indian independence in 1947. During the Raj, India was governed as a colony from England by a secretary of state for India and a council of India.

In India during this time, a governor general, more commonly referred to as the viceroy, served as the British government and as England's representative. He answered to the secretary of state for India and through him to the British king, prime minister, and parliament. There was also a Legislative Council that the viceroy worked with in India, half of which consisted of British officials with the power to vote on decisions, and half made up of Indians and English citizens living in India, who served only as advisers and could not vote. Although some Indians were appointed to the Legislative Council after the Revolt of 1857, these were mostly wealthy landowners, chosen for their loyalty to Britain, and hardly representative of the millions of Indian peasants.

Meanwhile, the Indian National Congress—or Congress, as it was simply called—began as a debating society in India in 1885. It was made up of wealthy Indians and Englishmen, loyal to the British Empire, and as such, it was largely ignored by the Raj. Its debates, however, helped provide a forum for discussion of the effects of Britain's presence in India and the rise of the rise of nationalist leaders.

Not wishing to be held responsible for the frail Indian leader's death while fasting, the viceroy offered to release Gandhi. Without recognition that he was certainly not to blame for the violence, Gandhi preferred to remain in prison and continue fasting. As biographer Chadha relates, "For the first two days Gandhi was quite cheerful, but on the third day he discontinued his morning and evening walks. On the eleventh day of the fast, it appeared that Gandhi would not survive. Kasturbai knelt before a sacred plant and prayed; she thought he was on the verge of breathing his last."[4]

But the Mahatma did not die. On the advice of doctors, a small amount of lime juice was added to his drinking water, and his condition improved. On March 3, the fast was concluded with the usual ceremonies—he drank a small amount of orange juice and performed a ritual of purification.

Kasturbai's health was failing, however, and in February 1944, she passed away in her husband's arms. The funeral rites were held the next day on the prison grounds where she had spent her last days with her husband, who grieved for her loss.

In the coming weeks the Mahatma himself suffered several illnesses, until in May 1944, when he and many other prisoners were released. When he left the Aga Khan Palace, it was the last prison he would leave. At that point, he had spent 2,089 days in prison in India, and before that, 249 days in prison in South Africa.[5]

He went to rest and recuperate from his fasts, personal losses, and illnesses at the homes of a series of friends. As his strength returned, he attempted to meet with the newest viceroy, Lord Wavell, and failing that, with the Muslim leader, Jinnah. While Gandhi had been in prison,

The Gandhis had no home of their own for many of their last years, staying with friends and supporters—when not in prison.

Jinnah had been negotiating the partition of India into two nations, one Muslim (Pakistan) and one Hindu (India). In addition, Jinnah wanted this division to take place before the British left India, not after, as Gandhi proposed, hoping it would not happen at all.

In the summer of 1945, as the Second World War drew to an end, it seemed clear that the days of British rule were numbered. Winston Churchill had been voted out as prime minister in England, and the new Labor government had an entirely different set of priorities. In September, the viceroy announced that a new executive council would be formed from all political parties in India to guide what he hoped would be a peaceful transition of power. What form of independence would take remained to be seen. Both the Indian National Congress and the Muslim League offered plans and counter plans, but neither side was willing to accept the other's proposals, and neither trusted the British to be fair to its cause.

In response to what he saw as the British favoring the Congress and Hindus, Jinnah called for a Direct Action Day on August 16, 1946, with the goal of achieving a Muslim-controlled Pakistan. As Gandhi biographer Chadha writes, on that day, and for three more days, the streets of Calcutta ran with blood following mass riots, leaving more than five thousand dead, at least twenty thousand seriously injured, and a hundred thousand residents homeless. After the first shock of Direct Action, the Hindu population of Calcutta organized and hit back with a parallel fury.[6]

Despite the carnage, the gradual withdrawal of British control and the transition of power to Indians that the British had planned moved forward. Nehru took office as prime minister of India on September 2, 1946. Jinnah's followers greeted the inauguration of the new Congress government with black flags of mourning. As the violence in the streets continued, Gandhi decided that he would travel to eastern Bengal, and specifically to Noakhali, where mass killings of Hindus were taking place. He traveled from Delhi to Calcutta, where he planned to meet with Prime Minister Nehru and rest before continuing into the fray.

Refugees from the violence in eastern Bengal were pouring into Calcutta with stories of terrible atrocities. In predominantly Hindu Bihar, thousands of Muslims were massacred in retaliation for previous attacks.

On November 6, Gandhi traveled into the Noakhali region from Calcutta. As he visited countless villages filled with hatred and outrage, and sent trusted followers into others, Gandhi spoke of fearlessness and forgiveness. He wrote to a friend that ahimsa was being tested here in a way it never had been before.

As Gandhi moved among the refugees, he found himself the target of criticism and threats from all directions. Muslims asked him why he did not go to Bihar and tend to Muslim victims of Hindu violence. The Hindu leaders in the Indian Congress were asking him to accept the reality of a divided India. The extent of the hostilities every way he turned left him feeling increasingly frustrated and despondent.

When what would be the last British viceroy, Lord Mountbatten, arrived in India in the spring of 1947, the continuing transfer of power on the Indian subcontinent was anything but peaceful. Despite the turmoil, England was determined to leave India to its masses as quickly as possible.

Thus, on August 15, 1947, the Dominion of Pakistan came into being with Muhammad Ali Jinnah as the governor general, as did the Union of India with Jawaharlal Nehru as the prime minister and Lord Mountbatten as the governor general. Even the official ceremonies were split, with those in Karachi, Pakistan, taking place one day before those in Delhi.

As William Dalrymple explains in the review of the book *The Great Divide*, partition led directly to "one of the greatest migrations in human history, as millions of Muslims trekked to West and East Pakistan (the latter now known as Bangladesh) while millions of Hindus and Sikhs headed in the opposite direction. Many hundreds of thousands never made it. In Punjab and Bengal—provinces abutting India's borders with West and East Pakistan—the carnage was especially intense, with massacres, arson, forced conversions, mass abductions, and savage sexual violence. By 1948, more than fifteen million people had been uprooted, and between one and two million were dead."[7]

9
The End of a Great Soul's Life

When the long-awaited independence of India arrived on August 15, 1947, amidst partition and genocide, it offered little for Mahatma Gandhi to celebrate. Since the announcement of Britain's post-war plans for a transition of power in India, most of the work of negotiating India's political future had been left to Nehru and the Congress. The larger picture of India's social future, especially as related to the khadi and Harijan movements, would be his focus. Gandhi spent Independence Day far from the ceremony in Delhi, spinning, fasting, and praying. When government officials asked him to make a statement, he replied that he "had run dry. There is no message at all."[1]

On his seventy-eighth birthday in October, well-wishers streamed into the house where he was staying, only to find the Mahatma tired and discouraged. He had once claimed that he wanted to live for 125 years. He had changed his mind. "I have lost all desire to live long," he now said.[2]

At a prayer meeting on January 12, 1948, he declared his intention to fast yet again "until there is a reunion of hearts of all communities, brought about not by outside pressure, but from an awakened sense of duty."[3]

Prime Minister Nehru delivers a speech at Parliament House in
New Delhi, August 15, 1947.

While he fasted, Gandhi insisted that India pay Pakistan the money it was owed as part of the partition, notwithstanding the violence taking place against Hindus and Sikhs in Pakistan. Not everyone felt this way. "Blood for blood," Hindu demonstrators shouted nearby the house where the Mahatma was fasting. Cries of "let Gandhi die" could also be heard.[4] Millions of Muslims distrusted Gandhi as a Hindu while many Hindus claimed that Gandhi had not fought hard enough for "their side." In truth, no one stood more steadfastly for Muslim-Hindu unity than Gandhiji.

Within three days of beginning this fast, Gandhi was showing signs of kidney failure, and his condition quickly worsened. So weak that a microphone had to be strapped to him, Gandhi spoke on All-India Radio saying, "Each of us should turn the searchlight inward and purify his or her heart as much as possible."[5]

Now pro-Gandhi demonstrators took to the streets, hoping to create peace between the communities that would end Gandhi's fast and prolong his life. A large crowd gathered outside the house where the leader beloved by so many lay on a cot. Prime Minister Nehru pleaded for peace in Delhi on behalf of the Mahatma.

THE TRIAL OF GANDHI'S ASSASSIN

Nathuram Godse, the man who fired three bullets into Gandhi's chest, provided testimony during his trial about his actions and the reasons behind them. He indicated that he did not personally hate Gandhi. In fact, he said, "Before I fired the shots, I wished him well and bowed to him in reverence."[6]

Godse and other militants like him believed that Gandhi was responsible for dividing the country into India and Pakistan, though this was clearly not the case. Godse and co-conspirator Narayan Apte were hanged for the murder of Mohandas Gandhi on November 15, 1949.

In a book titled *Freedom at Midnight*, researchers Larry Collins and Dominique Lapierre detailed how the conspiracy to kill Gandhi was planned and executed. The book reports that Gandhi's assassination was the outcome of a larger conspiracy by a group of Hindus determined to eliminate Gandhi from the political scene. Collins and Lapierre interviewed people who played key roles in the conspiracy, such as Nathuram's brother Gopal Godse, Vishnu Karkare, who assisted in hatching the plan, and Madanlal Pahwa, who unsuccessfully attempted to kill Gandhi ten days before the successful assassination.

As Aniket Alam, executive editor of *Economic and Political Weekly* explains, "There are two main understandings of Indian nationalism, one which considers Hinduism to be its central feature and the

Mourners climb telephone poles to view the funeral procession of their beloved Bapu, February 1948.

other which considers everyone who identifies with and adopts India to be Indian."[7] The conspirators were among those who firmly believed in India as a Hindu-led nation. Gandhi and Nehru sought a more inclusive India, and this was ultimately the reasoning behind the assassination.

Finally, in response to numerous pledges of ongoing unity, Gandhi agreed to end his fast on January 18. He wanted to leave Delhi and travel to blood-soaked Pakistan. He told his followers that his hopes to live to the age of 125 would be renewed if the pledges they'd made were truly honored and peace between the factions was maintained.

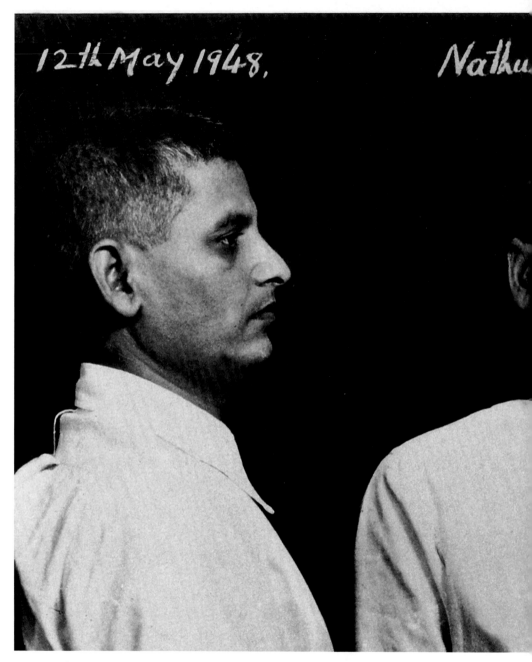

The man who, by his own admission, fired shots into the Mahatma's chest, killing him almost instantly

Vinayak Godse.

For the time being, however, he remained where he'd been staying at Birla House, the home of one of his followers, G. D. Birla. A few days later there was an explosion not far from where Gandhi was speaking to his followers. The young Hindu who had thrown a bomb was caught and arrested, though others that had been with him escaped. The security around Gandhi was tightened a bit, but he would not allow the police to search everyone who came to the prayer meetings.

On January 30, 1948, after a day spent spinning and discussing government matters, Gandhi walked as he always did toward the crowd gathered for the daily prayer meeting, supported on either side by young girls he called his "walking sticks." As the crowd parted to let him climb the steps to the prayer platform, Gandhi smiled and prayerfully touched his palms together. Suddenly, a young man stood in front of Gandhi and fired three shots directly into the spiritual leader's chest and abdomen. Police standing nearby quickly apprehended the shooter as the physically frail Mahatma collapsed on the ground, dying almost instantly, with the prayerful name of Rama on his lips.

When word spread throughout the crowd that "Bapuji" was dead, there were shouts of anger directed against Muslims. Fast thinking on the part of British Governor General Mountbatten, who'd arrived in anticipation of speaking with Gandhi after the prayer meeting, helped quell the immediate response by claiming, correctly as it turned out, that the shooter was in fact a Hindu.

Nehru was also at Birla House for a meeting with the Mahatma. Inside the house Nehru and Patel, who had been speaking with Gandhi about a disagreement between himself and Nehru just prior to Gandhi's departure for the prayer meeting, hugged each other in their mutual grief.

That evening Nehru spoke to the nation on All-India radio, saying, "The light has gone out of our lives." But then he corrected himself by adding that, "The light that has illumined this country for these many years will illumine it for many more years and a thousand years later that light will still be seen in this country and the world will see it and it will give solace to innumerable hearts."[8]

Before long, messages of condolence poured in from religious and political leaders around the world, including the presidents of the United States and France, the king of England, the pope, and the dalai lama. General George C. Marshall, the US secretary of state, spoke for many of the mourners when he said, "Mahatma Gandhi was the spokesman for the conscience of mankind."[9]

The next day, a funeral procession bore the Mahatma's body in an open casket from Birla House to the cremation pyre that had been constructed overnight. Author Arthur Herman relates that there were more than a million and a half people in the crowd that lined the funeral procession and waited near the pyre. A million more watched from rooftops all around.[10] The crowd chanted, "*Mahatma Gandhi amar ho gae*," which means "Mahatma Gandhi has become immortal," and the entire *Bhagavad Gita* was read.

> **"Not since Buddha has India so revered any man. Not since St. Francis of Assisi has any life known to history been so marked by gentleness, disinterestedness, simplicity of soul and forgiveness of enemies. We have the astonishing phenomenon of a revolution led by a saint."[11] —Will Durant, American historian**

The funeral was held on the shore of the Jumna River. Gandhi's youngest son, Devadas was there, and his third son, Ramdas, arrived in time to light the funeral pyre. Gandhi and Kasturbai's second son, Manilal, was in South Africa at the time. Sadly the oldest, Harilal, who had been estranged from his parents, only arrived late that night as smoke drifted from the ashes and would be dead himself a few months later of tuberculosis.

Many years later, Lord Mountbatten was interviewed about his time in India. The interviewers related, "We realized that this man who prided himself on being a professional warrior, a man who'd rolled over with his dying ship rather than leave his captain's bridge, was crying. Openly, unashamedly crying, as he described entering Birla House that January afternoon and seeing Gandhi's body laid out on his straw pallet."[12]

CONCLUSION

While Mohandas K. Gandhi is closely and rightfully associated with the birth of India as a free nation, he was deeply saddened by the violence that accompanied independence. And while his leadership helped bring an end to British colonial control of India, it is not likely that he would have called that his greatest achievement. His greatest achievement was his life itself. His greatest passion was the fight for the good of humanity. And his mightiest weapon was truth.

Gandhi worked to make things better for everyone, but especially the lowly. "All my life," he would say when he was very near the end of it, "I have stood, as everyone should stand, for minorities and those in need."[1] He tried to show that all religions, so long as they pursued a search for truth, or love, or God by any name, had value. His prayer meetings included readings from the holy works of Muslims, Christians, and Sikhs, as well as Hindus. His favorite hymns included both the "Vaishnava Jana" and "When I Survey the Wondrous Cross."[2]

Gandhi gave birth to satyagraha, a way of life that was different from all others. Far from being the last resort of the weak, as some have called other forms of passive resistance, for Gandhi, satyagraha required "the possession of unadulterated fearlessness."[3] Ahimsa, or nonviolence and *satya*, truth, were the twin pillars of satyagraha. And the deepest truth is that all life is one, and love is nonviolence in action. Holding to the truth of love, no matter how fierce the opposition, is both the ultimate goal and the means to that goal. This was taught by personal example.

His life, Gandhi said, was his message. After Gandhi's death, Philip Noel-Baker, British delegate to the United Nations, said, "his greatest accomplishments are still to come."[4]

The truth of that is evident in the lives of the great men and women who followed his example, as best they could, in the fight for humanity. A few of these include Khan Abdul Ghaffar Khan, in India; Nelson Mandela, in South Africa; and the Reverend Martin Luther King Jr., in the United States.

Khan Abdul Ghaffar Khan, also known as the "Frontier Gandhi," was a political and spiritual leader of the Pathans, a fierce Muslim people of the northwestern mountains of India. He was also a dedicated friend, supporter, and follower of Gandhi and satyagraha. He is credited with forming the "world's first nonviolent army," the Khudai Khidmatgars, or "Servants of God," in 1929, which numbered nearly one hundred thousand at the height of their struggle. [5]

Nelson Mandela, leader of the fight to end apartheid, was elected president of South Africa in 1994. Long after Mohandas Gandhi had left South Africa in 1914, the Natal Indian Congress that he had established helped influence the anti-apartheid movement. Though South African leader Nelson Mandela did not share Gandhi's unshakeable belief in the power of nonviolence in all cases, he was greatly inspired by Gandhi's efforts. As Gandhi scholar David Hardiman points out, Mandela never ceased regarding Gandhi as an inspiration. And Mandela learned from Gandhi the essential virtues of forgiveness and compassion, values that served him and his country very well when he became the first black African president of South Africa.[6]

In the United States, Reverend Martin Luther King Jr. became an important leader in the fight for civil rights for African Americans. From the early days of his political activism, King referred to Mahatma Gandhi as "the guiding light of our technique of nonviolent social change." In February 1959, King traveled to India, telling a group of reporters, "To other countries I may go as a tourist, but to India I come as a pilgrim."[7]

This trip would prove to have a profound influence on King's understanding of nonviolent resistance. Addressing a radio audience during his final evening in India, King stated:

> "[Since] being in India, I am more convinced than ever before that the method of nonviolent resistance is the most potent weapon available to oppressed people in their struggle for justice and human dignity. In a real sense, Mahatma Gandhi embodied in his life certain universal principles that are inherent in the moral structure of the universe, and these principles are as inescapable as the law of gravitation."[8]

The teachings of Gandhi continue to have powerful effects on leaders for social change in today's world. His Holiness the Dalai Lama, a world-renowned spiritual leader, and Aung San Suu Kyi, a recipient of the Nobel Peace Prize and a Burmese politician and activist, are two examples. In this way, Gandhi—and his struggles for peace through nonviolence—lives on.

CHRONOLOGY

1857 A revolt led by Indian soldiers results in transfer of control of India from the East India Company to the British crown. This is the beginning of the British Raj.

1869 Mohandas Karamchand Gandhi is born in Porbandar, India.

1882 Gandhi marries Kasturbai.

1885 Indian National Congress is founded.

1888 Gandhi sails to England to study law.

1891 Gandhi receives law credentials and returns to India.

1893 Gandhi is hired by Dada Abdulla and leaves India for South Africa; he experiences prejudice when his first-class train ticket is not honored and he is forced off a train in British Natal Colony.

1894 Gandhi establishes the Natal Indian Congress to fight discriminatory legislation.

1896 Gandhi returns briefly to India, publishes the Green Pamphlet, and brings his family back with him to South Africa.

1899 With the outbreak of the Boer War, Gandhi organizes the Indian Ambulance Corps to support the British cause.

1901 Gandhi and his family return to India; Gandhi attends a session of the Indian National Congress.

1902 The South African Indian Community requests Gandhi's assistance once again; Gandhi returns to Durban.

1903 Gandhi sets up a law practice in Johannesburg and begins publishing the *Indian Opinion*.

1904 Gandhi establishes the Phoenix Settlement and moves the production of the *Indian Opinion* there; he is joined in India by Kasturbai and their sons.

1906 Gandhi again supports the British cause during the Zulu Rebellion by forming an Indian Ambulance Corps; he launches nonviolent resistance against registration of Indians in the Transvaal and goes to England on behalf of South African Indians.

1907 Gandhi is arrested for his role in the registration resistance campaign.

1908 Gandhi is arrested and imprisoned multiple times; he burns his registration card after General Jan Smuts fails to repeal the Black Act.

1909 Gandhi is again arrested and imprisoned. He lobbies for South African Indians in England, corresponds with Tolstoy, and writes *Hind Swaraj* on return trip to South Africa.

1910 Gandhi establishes Tolstoy Farm near Johannesburg.

1913 Gandhi is imprisoned multiple times during the satyagraha against discriminatory Transvaal immigration laws.

1914 Gandhi reaches an agreement with General Smuts; he decides to return to India with his family but travels first, briefly, to England.